No Child Left Behind

A Parents Guide

No Child Left Behind
A Parents Guide

U.S. Department of Education

2003

THE SECRETARY OF EDUCATION
WASHINGTON, DC 20202

June 2003

Dear Parent:

On January 8, 2002, when the *No Child Left Behind Act* became the law of the land, we began a new era of education in our nation's history. Democrats and Republicans in Congress joined together with President Bush in an historic agreement to improve the educational opportunities for every American child.

Accountability, local control and flexibility, new options for parents, and record funding for what works are now the cornerstones of our education system. If your child isn't learning, you'll know why. If your school isn't performing, you'll have new options and the school will receive additional help. Our commitment to you, and to all Americans, is to see every child in America—regardless of ethnicity, income, or background—achieve high standards.

No Child Left Behind puts the focus on instruction and methods that have been proven to work. It makes a billion-dollar annual investment to ensure every child learns to read by third grade. And it provides the resources for reform and unprecedented flexibility so states and local communities can get the job done.

Everyone at the Department of Education is working hard in partnership with state and local leaders to implement the reforms of *No Child Left Behind*. We are already seeing great progress. From inner cities to sparsely populated rural areas and everywhere in between, we are pressing on toward our common goal of making every public school in America a place of high expectations and a place of high achievement.

This guide is meant to provide you with information about *No Child Left Behind*. It summarizes the main provisions of the law, answers common questions, and provides information on where you can find additional resources. I encourage you to share it with your family, friends, and neighbors.

President Bush and I believe in the bright hope of your child. As we move forward, our mission is clear: an America where every child will be educated and no child left behind.

Sincerely,

Rod Paige

Our mission is to ensure equal access to education and to promote educational excellence throughout the nation.

Contents

Introduction and Overview................................... 1
    No Child Left Behind—The Law That Ushered in a New Era...... 1
    What *No Child Left Behind* Does for Parents and Children....... 1
    Why *No Child Left Behind* Is Important to America............. 4
    United for Results.. 5

Questions and Answers on *No Child Left Behind*................ 7
    Accountability... 7
    Testing... 11
    Reading.. 15
    Doing What Works.. 18
    Teacher Quality... 20
    Creating Safer Schools...................................... 22
    Choice and Supplemental Educational Services................ 23
    Charter Schools... 25

Appendixes
    A. Where to Go for More Information........................ 27
    B. Titles of the *Elementary and Secondary Education Act of 1965*, as reauthorized by the *No Child Left Behind Act of 2001*........ 29
    C. Key Sections of Title I—Improving the Academic Achievement of the Disadvantaged, Pertaining to Parent Involvement..... 31
    D. Cited References... 37

Introduction and Overview

No Child Left Behind —The Law That Ushered in a New Era

The *No Child Left Behind Act of 2001* (*No Child Left Behind*) is a landmark in education reform designed to improve student achievement and change the culture of America's schools. President George W. Bush describes this law as the "cornerstone of my administration." Clearly, our children are our future, and, as President Bush has expressed, "Too many of our neediest children are being left behind."

With passage of *No Child Left Behind*, Congress reauthorized the *Elementary and Secondary Education Act (ESEA)*—the principal federal law affecting education from kindergarten through high school. In amending *ESEA*, the new law represents a sweeping overhaul of federal efforts to support elementary and secondary education in the United States. It is built on four common-sense pillars: accountability for results; an emphasis on doing what works based on scientific research; expanded parental options; and expanded local control and flexibility.

What *No Child Left Behind* Does for Parents and Children

Supports learning in the early years, thereby preventing many learning difficulties that may arise later

Children who enter school with language skills and pre-reading skills (e.g., understanding that print reads from left to right and top to bottom) are more likely to learn to read well in the early grades and succeed in later years. In fact, research shows that most reading problems faced by adolescents and adults are the result of problems that could have been prevented through good instruction in their early childhood years (Snow, Burns and Griffin 1998). It is never too early to start building language skills by talking with and reading to children. *No Child Left Behind* targets resources for early childhood education so that all youngsters get the right start.

Provides more information for parents about their child's progress

Under *No Child Left Behind*, each state must measure every public school student's progress in reading and math in each of grades 3 through 8 and at least once during grades 10 through 12. By school year 2007-2008, assessments (or testing) in science will be underway. These assessments must be aligned with state academic content and achievement standards. They will provide parents with objective data on where their child stands academically.

Alerts parents to important information on the performance of their child's school

No Child Left Behind requires states and school districts to give parents easy-to-read, detailed report cards on schools and districts, telling them which ones are succeeding and why. Included in the report cards are student achievement data broken out by race, ethnicity, gender, English language proficiency, migrant status, disability status and low-income status; as well as important information about the professional qualifications of teachers. With these provisions, *No Child Left Behind* ensures that parents have important, timely information about the schools their children attend—whether they are performing well or not for *all* children, regardless of their background.

Gives children and parents a lifeline

In this new era of education, children will no longer be trapped in the dead end of low-performing schools. Under *No Child Left Behind,* such schools must use their federal funds to make needed improvements. In the event of a school's continued poor performance, parents have options to ensure that their children receive the high-quality education to which they are entitled. That might mean that children can transfer to higher-performing schools in the area or receive supplemental educational services in the community, such as tutoring, after-school programs or remedial classes.

Improves teaching and learning by providing better information to teachers and principals

Annual tests to measure children's progress provide teachers with independent information about each child's strengths and weaknesses. With this knowledge, teachers can craft lessons to make sure each student meets or exceeds the standards. In addition, principals can use the data to assess exactly how much progress each teacher's students have made and to better inform decisions about how to run their schools.

Ensures that teacher quality is a high priority

No Child Left Behind defines the qualifications needed by teachers and paraprofessionals who work on any facet of classroom instruction. It requires that states develop plans to achieve the goal that all teachers of core academic subjects be highly qualified by the end of the 2005-06 school year. States must include in their plans annual, measurable objectives that each local school district* and school must meet in moving toward the goal; they must report on their progress in the annual report cards.

Gives more resources to schools

Today, more than $7,000 on average is spent per pupil by local, state and federal taxpayers. States and local school districts are now receiving more federal funding than ever before for all programs under *No Child Left Behind*: $23.7 billion, most of which will be used during the 2003-04 school year. This represents an increase of 59.8 percent from 2000 to 2003. A large portion of these funds is for grants under Title I of *ESEA*: Improving the Academic Achievement of the Disadvantaged. Title I grants are awarded to states and local education agencies to help states and school districts improve the education of disadvantaged students; turn around low-performing schools; improve teacher quality; and increase choices for parents. (For more about Title I, see the introductory paragraph to Q-and-As on page 7.) For fiscal year (FY) 2003, funding for Title I alone is $11.7 billion—an increase of 33 percent since the passage of *No Child Left Behind*. President Bush's FY 2004 budget request would increase spending on Title I by 48 percent since he took office.

Allows more flexibility

In exchange for the strong accountability, *No Child Left Behind* gives states and local education agencies more flexibility in the use of their federal education funding. As a result, principals and administrators spend less time filling out forms and dealing with federal red tape. They have more time to devote to students' needs. They have more freedom to implement innovations and allocate resources as policymakers at the state and local levels see fit, thereby giving local people a greater opportunity to affect decisions regarding their schools' programs.

Focuses on what works

No Child Left Behind puts a special emphasis on implementing educational programs and practices that have been clearly demonstrated to be effective through rigorous scientific research. Federal funding will be targeted to support such programs. For example, the Reading First program makes federal funds available to help reading teachers in the early grades strengthen old skills and gain new ones in instructional techniques that scientifically based research has shown to be effective.

---

*Note: For the purpose of discussion in this book, the terms " district" and "local education agency" are used interchangeably in discussing the agency at the local level responsible for maintaining administrative control of public elementary and secondary schools in a given area or political subdivision of the state.

Why *No Child Left Behind* Is Important to America

Federal Spending on K-12 Education under the *Elementary and Secondary Education Act* and NAEP Reading Scores (Age 9)

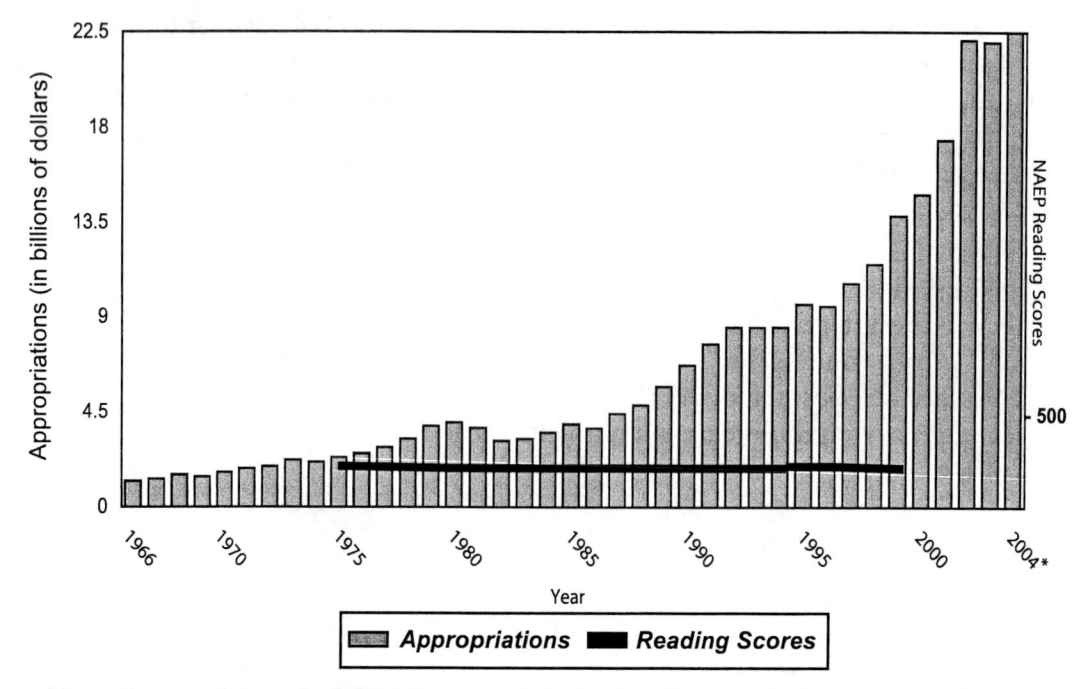

Note: Appropriations for *ESEA* do not include funding for special education. Reading scores are the average scores for 9-year-olds, according to the National Assessment of Educational Progress (NAEP). A score of 200 implies an ability to understand, combine ideas and make inferences based on short, uncomplicated passages about specific or sequentially related information.

*Reflects the President's budget request for 2004.

Source: U.S. Department of Education Budget Service and *NAEP 1999 Trends in Academic Progress*.

Since the *Elementary and Secondary Education Act* first passed Congress in 1965, the federal government has spent more than $242 billion through 2003 to help educate disadvantaged children. Yet, the achievement gap in this country between rich and poor and white and minority students remains wide. According to the most recent National Assessment of Educational Progress (NAEP) on reading in 2000, only 32 percent of fourth-graders can read at a proficient level and thereby demonstrate solid academic achievement; and while scores for the highest-performing students have improved over time, those of America's lowest-performing students have declined (National Assessment of Educational Progress 2001).

The good news is that some schools in cities and towns across the nation are creating high achievement for children with a history of low performance. If some schools can do it, then all schools should be able to do it.

United for Results

Because of *No Child Left Behind*:

Parents will know their children's strengths and weaknesses and how well schools are performing; they will have other options and resources for helping their children if their schools are chronically in need of improvement.

Teachers will have the training and resources they need for teaching effectively, using curricula that are grounded in scientifically based research; annual testing lets them know areas in which students need extra attention.

Principals will have information they need to strengthen their schools' weaknesses and to put into practice methods and strategies backed by sound, scientific research.

Superintendents will be able to see which of their schools and principals are doing the best job and which need help to improve.

School boards will be able to measure how their districts are doing and to measure their districts in relation to others across the state; they will have more and better information on which to base decisions about priorities in their districts.

Chief state school officers will know how the schools in their states and in other states are doing; they will be better able to pinpoint where guidance and resources are needed.

Governors will have a yearly report card on how their states' schools are doing; they will be able to highlight accomplishments of the best schools and target help to those schools that are in need of improvement.

Community leaders and volunteer groups will have information they can use to rally their members in efforts to help children and schools that need the most help.

Questions and Answers on *No Child Left Behind*

The following discussion pertains only to public schools. Please note that the term "Title I schools" refers to those schools that receive funds under Title I of the *Elementary and Secondary Education Act (ESEA)*: Improving the Academic Achievement of the Disadvantaged. Title I supports programs to improve the academic achievement of children of low-income families. Currently, about half (55 percent) of public schools receive funds under Title I.

Accountability

How are school report cards put together and what kind of information do they provide?

Reports on individual schools are part of the annual district report cards, also known as local report cards. Each school district must prepare and disseminate annual local report cards that include information on how students in the district and in each school performed on state assessments. The report cards must state student performance in terms of three levels: basic, proficient and advanced. Achievement data must be disaggregated, or broken out, by student subgroups according to: race, ethnicity, gender, English language proficiency, migrant status, disability status and low-income status. The report cards must also tell which schools have been identified as needing improvement, corrective action or restructuring (defined in Q-and-A below: "What if a school does not improve?").

How can parents see these local report cards, which include school-by-school data?

States must ensure that the local districts make these local report cards available to the parents of students promptly and by no later than the beginning of the school year. The law requires that the information be presented in an "understandable and uniform format, and to the extent practicable, in a language that the parents can understand." States and districts may also distribute this information to the media for publicizing; post it on the Internet; or provide it to other public agencies for dissemination.

Further, local school districts must notify parents if their child's school has been identified as needing improvement, corrective action or restructuring (defined in Q-and-A below: "What if a school does not improve?"). In this event, districts must let parents know the options available to them (see section on Choice and Supplemental Educational Services on page 23). Also, districts must annually notify parents of students in Title I schools of their "right to know" about teacher qualifications and how to exercise it (see section on Teacher Quality on page 20).

What information is provided on state report cards?

Each state must produce and disseminate annual report cards that provide information on student achievement in the state—both overall and broken out according to the same subgroups as those appearing on the district report cards listed above. State report cards include:

- State assessment results by performance level (basic, proficient and advanced), including (1) two-year trend data for each subject and grade tested; and (2) a comparison between annual objectives and actual performance for each student group.

- Percentage of each group of students not tested.

- Graduation rates for secondary school students and any other student achievement indicators that the state chooses.

- Performance of school districts on adequate yearly progress measures, including the number and names of schools identified as needing improvement.

- Professional qualifications of teachers in the state, including the percentage of teachers in the classroom with only emergency or provisional credentials and the percentage of classes in the state that are *not* taught by highly qualified teachers, including a comparison between high- and low-income schools.

What is "adequate yearly progress"? How does measuring it help to improve schools?

No Child Left Behind requires each state to define adequate yearly progress for school districts and schools, within the parameters set by Title I. In defining adequate yearly progress, each state sets the minimum levels of improvement—measurable in terms of student performance—that school districts and schools must achieve within time frames specified in the law. In general, it works like this: Each state begins by setting a "starting point" that is based on the performance of its lowest-achieving demographic group or of the lowest-achieving schools in the state, whichever is higher. The state then sets the bar—or level of student achievement—that a school must attain after two years in order to continue to show adequate yearly progress. Subsequent thresholds must be raised at least once every three years, until, at the end of 12 years, all students in the state are achieving at the proficient level on state assessments in reading/language arts and math.

What if a school does not improve?

States and local school districts will aid schools that receive Title I funds in making meaningful changes that will improve their performance. In the meantime, districts will offer parents options for children in low-performing schools, including extra help to children from low-income families (see section on Choice and Supplemental Educational Services on page 23).

The *No Child Left Behind Act* lays out an action plan and timetable for steps to be taken when a Title I school fails to improve, as follows:

- A Title I school that has not made adequate yearly progress, as defined by the state, for two consecutive school years will be identified by the district before the beginning of the next school year as *needing improvement*. School officials will develop a two-year plan to turn around the school. The local education agency will ensure that the school receives needed technical assistance as it develops and implements its improvement plan. Students must be offered the option of transferring to another public school in the district—which may include a public charter school—that has not been identified as needing school improvement.

- If the school does not make adequate yearly progress for three years, the school remains in school-improvement status, and the district must continue to offer public school choice to all students. In addition, students from low-income families are eligible to receive supplemental educational services, such as tutoring or remedial classes, from a state-approved provider.

- If the school fails to make adequate progress for four years, the district must implement certain *corrective actions* to improve the school, such as replacing certain staff or fully implementing a new curriculum, while continuing to offer public school choice and supplemental educational services for low-income students.

- If a school fails to make adequate yearly progress for a fifth year, the school district must initiate plans for *restructuring* the school. This may include reopening the school as a charter school, replacing all or most of the school staff or turning over school operations either to the state or to a private company with a demonstrated record of effectiveness.

In addition, the law requires states to identify for improvement those local education agencies that fail to make adequate yearly progress for two consecutive years or longer and to institute corrective actions.

How are teachers or schools that do well rewarded?

No Child Left Behind requires states to provide state academic achievement awards to schools that close achievement gaps between groups of students or that exceed academic achievement goals. States may also use Title I funds to financially reward teachers in schools that receive academic achievement awards. In addition, states must designate as distinguished schools those that have made the greatest gains in closing the achievement gap or in exceeding achievement goals.

What can parents do to help their child's school succeed and meet the accountability requirements? How does the law help parents become involved?

No Child Left Behind supports parent involvement because research overwhelmingly demonstrates the positive effect that parent involvement has on their children's academic achievement (Clark 1983; Comer 1980, 1988; Eccles, Arbreton, et al., 1993; Eccles-Parsons, Adler and Kaczala 1982; Epstein 1983, 1984; Marjoribanks 1979 as cited in Eccles and Harold 1996). In the event a school is identified as needing improvement, corrective action or restructuring, the law requires the local education agency to notify parents accordingly and to explain to them how they can become involved in school-improvement efforts. In any event, the law requires the same agency to provide parents with local report cards, which include data on each individual school in the district, as described earlier. Thus, parents have up-to-date information about their child's school, which they can use in whatever manner they choose to be involved. Parents may help their child's school in a number of ways, including: attending parent-teacher meetings or special meetings to address academic problems at the school; volunteering to serve as needed; encouraging other parents to become involved; and learning about the school's special challenges, community resources and the *No Child Left Behind Act*. In addition, parents should take advantage of the increased flexibility given local decision-makers by *No Child Left Behind* and talk with their school board members, principals and other state and local education leaders about which programs they think will help their students the most.

The law has other specific requirements on parent involvement that include the following:

- Each state education agency must support the collection and dissemination of information on effective parent involvement practices to local education agencies and schools.

- The law in Title I spells out specific measures that local education agencies and schools receiving Title I funds must take to ensure parent involvement in significant areas, including: overall planning at the district and school levels; written policies on parent involvement at both levels; annual meetings; training; coordinating parent involvement strategies among federal education programs (i.e., Title I, Head Start and Reading First); and evaluating those strategies and revising them if needed. (Because this provision of the statute—Section 1118—is so important to effective parent involvement, it is reprinted at the end of this booklet on page 31).

- Schools that have schoolwide programs must involve parents in developing plans for such programs—that is, programs designed to raise the achievement of low-achieving students in high-poverty Title I schools by improving instruction throughout the entire school (thus using Title I funds to serve all children).

- The law provides for involvement of parents of private schools students served by various federal education programs such as Title I.

For more information on the four parent-involvement requirements mentioned above, see Appendix C: Key Sections of Title I—Improving the Academic Achievement of the Disadvantaged, Pertaining to Parent Involvement on page 31.

Testing

What impact does testing have on children?

Although testing may be stressful for some students, testing is a normal and expected way of assessing what students have learned. The purpose of state assessments required under *No Child Left Behind* is to provide an independent insight into each child's progress, as well as each school's. This information is essential for parents, schools, districts and states in their efforts to ensure that no child—regardless of race, ethnic group, gender or family income—is trapped in a consistently low-performing school.

Will student results be made available to parents?

Yes. State assessments will produce reports on each student that will be given to parents.

Will the results of a child's tests be private?

Absolutely. Only the parents and school receive the results of an individual child's tests. Individual student scores will not be made public. They are not a part of student achievement data on report cards issued by districts and states.

On what subjects are students tested and when?

No Child Left Behind requires that, by the 2005-06 school year, each state must measure every child's progress in reading and math in each of grades 3 through 8 and at least once during grades 10 through 12. In the meantime, each state must meet the requirements of the previous law reauthorizing *ESEA* (the *Improving America's Schools Act of 1994*) for assessments in reading and math at three grade spans (3-5; 6-9; and 10-12). By school year 2007-2008, states must also have in place science assessments to be administered at least once during grades 3-5; grades 6-9; and grades 10-12. Further, states must ensure that districts administer tests of English proficiency—to measure oral language, reading and writing skills in English—to all limited English proficient students, as of the 2002-03 school year.

Students may still undergo state assessments in other subject areas (i.e., history, geography and writing skills), if and when the state requires it. *No Child Left Behind*, however, requires assessments only in the areas of reading/language arts, math and science.

How is testing handled for children with disabilities? How is it handled for those with limited English proficiency?

No Child Left Behind requires that all children be assessed. In order to show adequate yearly progress, schools must test at least 95 percent of the various subgroups of children, including their students with disabilities and those with limited English proficiency. States must provide reasonable accommodations for students with disabilities or limited English proficiency. For the latter, accommodations may include native-language versions of the assessment; however, in the area of reading and language arts, students who have been in U.S. schools for three consecutive years will be assessed in English.
For more information on accommodations in a particular state, contact the appropriate state education agency.

Some say that testing causes teachers to teach to the test. Is that true?

State assessments are expected to measure how well students meet the state's academic *standards*, which define what students should know and be able to do in different subject areas at different grade levels. Under the previous reauthorization of the *Elementary and Secondary Education Act* in 1994, states were required to develop or adopt standards in mathematics and in reading or language arts; *No Child Left Behind* requires states to do the same with science standards by 2006. Curriculum based on state standards should be taught in the classroom. If teachers cover subject matter required by the standards and teach it well, then students will master the material on which they will be tested—and probably much more. In that case, students will need no special test preparation in order to do well.

Nevertheless, state assessments sound like they could take a lot of time and effort. What will be gained?

The point of state assessments is to measure student learning. A key principle of quality management is the importance of measuring what is valued (e.g., production rates; costs of materials, etc.). Such measures enable an organization to identify where and how to improve operations. In the same manner, if schools and school systems are to continuously improve, they must measure growth in student achievement. After all, the core of all activity in schools and school systems is teaching and learning, and the key question is: Are the students learning?

Do tests measure the progress of schools?

Annual state assessments required under *No Child Left Behind* produce data on student performance at individual schools; and this information is used to gauge whether each and every school is meeting the state's standard of "adequate yearly progress." Parents can check progress made in improving student performance at their child's school by checking the annual district report card. (See above section on Accountability.) If their school is *not* making adequate yearly progress and has been identified as needing improvement, corrective action or restructuring, *No Child Left Behind* requires that districts notify parents and offer options. (See section on Choice and Supplemental Educational Services on page 23.)

How does testing help teachers?

Annual testing provides teachers with a great deal of information. For example, overall poor results could indicate that the curriculum needs to be reviewed and aligned with the content upon which state standards are based; poor results could also mean that teachers need to modify their instructional methods. Another likely indicator of the same problems would be if teachers saw poor performance by their students in certain areas. Test results could also help teachers to clarify those areas in which they may need professional development. Finally, teachers gain a great deal of information about the performance of individual students that enables them to meet the particular needs of every child.

How does testing help principals?

Annual tests show principals exactly how much progress each teacher's students have made. They can use this information to guide decisions about program selection, curriculum arrangement, professional development for teachers and school resources they might need. Tests also show principals the strengths and weaknesses of students—in terms of the whole school, various subgroups and as individuals—and enable them to make plans that bolster strengths and address weaknesses.

How can parents find out if their child's school uses information gathered from testing to improve teaching and learning?

Parents can ask the principal how their school makes decisions about teaching and learning. They can ask such questions as: Does the faculty meet regularly; review performance data; and identify weaknesses to be targeted? Do programs and curricula follow state content standards defining what students should know and be able to do in a given subject, at a given grade level? How is the school using test data to guide decisions about teaching and learning (e.g., how do those data influence professional development, tutoring, and selection of materials)? Is there a schoolwide plan that uses testing to evaluate performance, determine areas of strengths and weaknesses in instruction and respond to targeted needs of students? Have test data revealed weaknesses at the school (e.g., low math scores in the fifth and sixth grades)? What are the teachers and principal doing to assess such problems and address them? These are important questions for parents to ask about how their child's school is using testing and the data obtained from it.

What about the National Assessment of Educational Progress (NAEP)?

Since 1969, NAEP has been the only nationally representative and continuing assessment of what American students know and can do in major academic subjects. Over the years NAEP has measured students' achievement in many subjects, including reading, mathematics, science, writing, history, civics, geography and the arts. Since 1992, the current NAEP reading assessment has been given in four different years (1992, 1994, 1998 and 2000) to a nationally representative sample of fourth-grade students. NAEP provides a wealth of data about the condition of education in the United States.

Under *No Child Left Behind*, as a condition of receiving federal funding, states are required to participate in the NAEP math and reading assessments for fourth- and eighth-grade students every two years, beginning in 2002-03. Resulting data will significantly increase information that parents—and others—can use to compare the performance of children in one state with that of children in another state. To carry it one step further, NAEP data will highlight the rigor of standards and tests for individual states: If there is a large discrepancy between children's proficiency on a state's tests and their performance on NAEP, that would suggest that the state needs to take a closer look at its standards and assessments and consider making improvements.

Reading

What's the current situation—how well are America's children reading?

Our students are not reading nearly well enough. As mentioned earlier, results of the most recent National Assessment of Educational Progress on reading showed that only 32 percent of the nation's fourth-graders performed at or above the proficient achievement level, thus demonstrating solid academic performance. And, while scores for the highest-performing students have improved over time, those of America's lowest-performing students have declined (National Assessment of Educational Progress 2001).

What is the key to turning this situation around?

Research has consistently identified the critical skills that young students need to learn in order to become good readers (National Reading Panel 2000). Teachers across different states and districts have demonstrated that scientifically based reading instruction can and does work with all children. They have taught children—even those among the most difficult to educate—to become proficient readers by the end of third grade. Thus, the key to helping all children learn is to help teachers in each and every classroom benefit from the relevant research. That can be accomplished by providing professional development for teachers on the use of scientifically based reading programs; by the use of instructional materials and programs that are also based on sound scientific research; and by ensuring accountability through ongoing assessments.

Why is it so important for children to learn good reading skills in the early years of school?

Research shows that children who read well in the early grades are far more successful in later years; and those who fall behind often stay behind when it comes to academic achievement (Snow, Burns and Griffin 1998). Reading opens the door to learning about math, history, science, literature, geography and much more. Thus, young, capable readers can succeed in these subjects, take advantage of other opportunities (such as reading for pleasure) and develop confidence in their own abilities. On the other hand, those students who cannot read well are much more likely to drop out of school and be limited to low-paying jobs throughout their lives. Reading is undeniably critical to success in today's society.

What is being done to help children learn to read well by the end of the third grade?

Improving the reading skills of children is a top priority for leaders at all levels of government and business, as well as for parents, teachers and countless citizens who volunteer at reading programs across the nation. At the national level, *No Child Left Behind* reflects this concern with the new program called Reading First. It is an ambitious national initiative designed to help every young child in every state become a successful reader. It is based on the expectation that instructional decisions for all students will be guided by the best available research. In recent years, scientific research has provided tremendous insight into exactly how children learn to read and the essential components for effective reading instruction. Reading First builds on this solid foundation of research.

How does Reading First work, and what are the specific goals?

Under Reading First, states can receive significant federal funding to improve reading achievement. In 2003 alone, almost $994 million is available for this program. These funds are specifically dedicated to helping states and local school districts establish high-quality, comprehensive reading instruction for all children in kindergarten through third grade. High-quality programs are, by definition, based on solid scientific research.

Awards for Reading First follow a straightforward, two-step process:

- First, each state applies for Reading First money that is then distributed on the basis of the number of low-income children aged 5-17 who live in the state. A major way in which states use their funds is to organize a scientifically based professional development program for all teachers, in grades K-3.

- The bulk of state funds, however, go to districts and schools to meet students' instructional needs. Districts with the greatest needs compete for funds in state-run competitions, with priority given to those with high rates of poverty and reading failure. Once funds reach the districts, Reading First monies are flexible and can be used for diagnostic assessments to determine which students in grades K-3 are at risk of reading failure; for teacher professional development; to purchase reading materials; and for ongoing support to improve reading instruction.

Through Reading First, funds are made available for state and local early reading programs that are grounded in scientifically based research. In such programs, students are systematically and explicitly taught the following five skills identified by research as critical to early reading success. The definitions below are from the *Report of the National Reading Panel* (2000):

- *Phonemic awareness*: the ability to hear and identify sounds in spoken words.

- *Phonics*: the relationship between the letters of written language and the sounds of spoken language.

- *Fluency*: the capacity to read text accurately and quickly.

- *Vocabulary*: the words students must know to communicate effectively.

- *Comprehension*: the ability to understand and gain meaning from what has been read.

How will we know if Reading First is working?

Information to make that judgment will come from the states. *No Child Left Behind* requires each state to: (1) prepare an annual report showing the greatest gains in reading achievement; (2) reduce the number of children in grades 1-3 who are reading below grade level; and (3) increase the percentage of children overall who are reading at grade level or above. In order to fulfill these requirements, states must measure progress in reading skills for children in grades 1-2; and, as prescribed by *No Child Left Behind*, states have to ensure that all children in grades 3-8 are tested annually in reading. Results of these assessments should soon provide clear evidence of Reading First's effectiveness. There is good cause for confidence, since the programs and practices that Reading First supports must already have been demonstrated as effective, based on solid scientific research.

Does *No Child Left Behind* support programs to help children build language and pre-reading skills before they start kindergarten?

Yes. Early Reading First supports preschool programs that provide a high-quality education to young children, especially those from low-income families. While early childhood programs are important for children's social, emotional and physical development, they are also important for children's early cognitive and language development. Research stresses the importance of early reading skills, including phonemic awareness and vocabulary development, as described above. Early Reading First supports programs to help preschoolers improve these skills. These programs can include professional development of staff and identifying and providing activities and instructional material. Programs must be grounded in scientifically based research, and their success must continually be evaluated.

Doing What Works

There are a lot of education fads. Does *No Child Left Behind* do anything to prevent bad or untested programs from being used in the classroom?

For too many years, too many schools have experimented with lessons and materials that have proven to be ineffective—at the expense of their students. Under *No Child Left Behind*, federal support is targeted to those educational programs that have been demonstrated to be effective through rigorous scientific research. Reading First is such a program. Programs and practices grounded in scientifically based research are not fads or untested ideas; they have proven track records of success. By funding such programs, *No Child Left Behind* encourages their use, as opposed to the use of untried programs that may later turn out to be fads. Furthermore, *No Child Left Behind's* accountability requirements bring real consequences to those schools that continually fail to improve student achievement as a result of using programs and practices for which there is no evidence of success. Such schools would be identified as needing improvement and required to make changes as outlined in the section on Accountability, including using education programs that are grounded in scientifically based research.

What is scientifically based research?

To say that an instructional program or practice is grounded in scientifically based research means there is reliable evidence that the program or practice works. For example, to obtain reliable evidence about a reading strategy or instructional practice, an experimental study may be done that involves using an experimental/control group design to see if the method is effective in teaching children to read.

No Child Left Behind sets forth rigorous requirements to ensure that research is scientifically based. It moves the testing of educational practices toward the medical model used by scientists to assess the effectiveness of medications, therapies and the like. Studies that test random samples of the population and that involve a control group are scientifically controlled. To gain scientifically based research about a particular educational program or practice, it must be the subject of such a study. Going back to the example of reading: *No Child Left Behind* requires that Reading First support those programs that teach children five skills (phonemic awareness, phonics, fluency, vocabulary and comprehension). These skills have been shown to be critical to early reading success through years of scientifically based research on the practice of reading instruction. In April 2000, these research findings were reported in the congressionally mandated National Reading Panel report mentioned earlier; they have now been written into the new law.

How can parents find out about scientifically based research that applies to federal education programs, aside from the research on reading?

In 2002, the Department of Education's Institute of Education Sciences (IES) established the What Works Clearinghouse to provide a central, independent and trusted source of scientific evidence on what works in education for parents, educators, policymakers and anyone else who is interested. All of the research collected and conducted by the clearinghouse follows the same high scientific standards as those used for reading research and will be available via the Internet from the clearinghouse or through the Department's Web site. (See Appendix A: Where to Go for More Information on page 27). Parents may be able to use this information to find out about program and curricula selection at their child's school. The seven topics chosen for systematic review in the first year of the What Works Clearinghouse's operation reflect a wide range of our nation's most pressing education issues. They are:

- Interventions for Beginning Reading;

- Curriculum-based Interventions for Increasing K-12 Math Achievement;

- High School Dropout Prevention;

- Peer-Assisted Learning in Elementary Schools: Reading, Mathematics and Science Gains;

- Programs for Increasing Adult Literacy;

- Interventions to Reduce Delinquent, Disorderly and Violent Behavior, in and out of School; and

- Interventions for Elementary English Language Learners: Increasing English Language Acquisition and Academic Achievement.

Over time, as the clearinghouse begins to produce its reports on these issues, parents will be able to ask their principal, teachers and school board members about the extent to which they select programs and curricula that the research has determined to be effective. Under *No Child Left Behind*, educators are expected to consider the results of relevant scientifically based research—whenever such information is available—before making instructional decisions.

Teacher Quality

How does this law improve teacher quality?

No Child Left Behind requires local school districts to ensure that all teachers hired to teach core academic subjects in Title I programs after the first day of the 2002-03 school year are highly qualified. In general a "highly qualified teacher" is one with full certification, a bachelor's degree and demonstrated competence in subject knowledge and teaching. (Core subjects include English, reading or language arts, mathematics, science, foreign languages, civics and government, economics, arts, history and geography.) The act also calls for *all* teachers of the core academic subjects (teaching in Title II programs or elsewhere) to be highly qualified by the end of school year 2005-06.

No Child Left Behind (*ESEA*, Title II) provides federal funding to states and districts for activities that will strengthen teacher quality in all schools, especially those with a high proportion of children in poverty. The great majority of Title II funds, $2.9 billion in 2003—an increase of 39 percent since President Bush took office—is for the Improving Teacher Quality State Grants program. Funding can be used to support a wide array of activities, including interventions for teacher professional development, so long as the activities are grounded in scientifically based research. Because communities nationwide face such a variety of needs when it comes to teacher quality, the law gives schools and districts a great deal of flexibility in how the money is spent. It also holds them accountable for the proper and effective use of the funds.

In addition to the state grants program, Title II includes funding for other teacher quality-related grant programs. For example, this year the Transition to Teaching program will allocate nearly $42 million to states, school districts and nonprofit groups to help thousands of outstanding candidates enter teaching through alternate routes to traditional teacher preparation programs. Similarly, Troops to Teachers, which helps states and school districts streamline the entry of former military personnel into schools as teachers, will receive almost $29 million in funding. The Teaching of Traditional American History grant program will allocate almost $100 million this year to states, school districts and education groups to help improve, through teacher professional development, the quality and rigor of American history instruction in the nation's schools. *No Child Left Behind* also requires districts to spend Title I funds to improve teacher quality and allows them to pool other federal formula funds and use them for that purpose.

How are states and districts held accountable for improving teacher quality?

Each state that receives Title II funds must develop a plan to ensure that all teachers of core academic subjects are highly qualified by the end of the 2005-06 school year. The plan must establish annual, measurable objectives for each local school district and school to ensure that they meet the "highly qualified" requirement.

In schools that receive funds under Title II, principals must make a statement each year as to whether the school is in compliance with the "highly qualified" teacher requirement. This information will be maintained at the school and district offices where members of the public can see it upon request. In addition, each school district must report to the state annually on its progress in meeting the requirement that all teachers be "highly qualified" by the end of the 2005-06 school year. This information is part of the state report cards described earlier.

How can parents find out about the quality of their child's teachers?

Parents of students in Title I schools are guaranteed annual notification of their "right to know" about teacher qualifications by their school district. That means parents may request and receive from that office information regarding the professional qualifications of the student's classroom teachers, including: (a) whether a teacher is state-certified; (b) whether a teacher is teaching under emergency or other provisional status; and (c) the baccalaureate degree major of a teacher and any other graduate degree major or certification.

What about paraprofessionals or teachers' aides? Does *No Child Left Behind* call for increased academic requirements for them?

While paraprofessionals or teachers' aides are valuable assets to many learning communities, they are not qualified to fill the role of teachers—a role which, unfortunately, many have been called upon to fill, especially in schools that are under-staffed. *No Child Left Behind* is clear that teachers' aides may provide instructional services only under the direct supervision of a teacher. In addition, the law allows teachers' aides to facilitate instruction only if they have met certain academic requirements: They must have at least an associate's degree or two years of college, or they must meet a rigorous standard of quality through a formal state or local assessment. If a paraprofessional's role does not involve facilitating instruction—such as serving as a hall monitor—that person does not have to meet the same academic requirements. But, in order to provide instructional services, an aide or paraprofessional must have the academic background required by *No Child Left Behind*.

Why is teacher quality such an important issue?

A major objective of *No Child Left Behind* is to ensure high-quality teachers for all students, regardless of race, ethnicity or income, because a well-prepared teacher is vitally important to a child's education. In fact, research demonstrates the clear correlation between student academic achievement and teacher quality (Sanders and Rivers 1996). Parents should never hesitate to inquire within their school and district about the qualifications of teachers instructing their children.

Creating Safer Schools

How big a problem is crime in schools?

In 2000, students ages 12 through 18 were victims of about 2 million crimes at school, including about 128,000 serious violent crimes (including rape, sexual assault, robbery and aggravated assault). That same year, about 29 percent of students in grades 9 through 12 reported that someone had offered, sold or given them an illegal drug on school property. While overall school crime rates have declined over the last few years, violence, gangs and drugs are still present, indicating that more work needs to be done.

How can parents find out about safety at their child's school?

Under Title IV of *ESEA* as reauthorized by the *No Child Left Behind Act,* states are required to establish a uniform management and reporting system to collect information on school safety and drug use among young people. The states must include incident reports by school officials and anonymous student and teacher surveys in the data they collect. This information is to be publicly reported so that parents, school officials and others who are interested have information about any violence and drug use at their schools. They can then assess the problems at their schools and work toward finding solutions. Continual monitoring and reports will track progress over time.

How can schools be made safer?

Title IV provides support for programs to prevent violence in and around schools; prevent the illegal use of alcohol, drug and tobacco by young people; and foster a safe and drug-free learning environment that supports academic achievement. Most of the funds are awarded to states, which, in turn, award money to the districts for a wide range of drug- and violence-prevention programs. These programs must address local needs as determined by objective data and be grounded in scientifically based prevention activities. They must also involve parents. The effectiveness of these programs must be continuously measured and evaluated.

What can be done immediately for students who are in unsafe schools?

Parents of children who have been the victims of a violent crime at school or who attend "persistently dangerous schools"—as determined by the state—will be offered school choice, as described in the next section.

Choice and Supplemental Educational Services

When are children eligible for school choice?

Children are eligible for school choice when the Title I school they attend has not made adequate yearly progress in improving student achievement—as defined by the state—for two consecutive years or longer and is therefore identified as needing improvement, corrective action or restructuring. Any child attending such a school must be offered the option of transferring to a public school in the district—including a public charter school—not identified for school improvement, unless such an option is prohibited by state law. *No Child Left Behind* requires that priority in providing school choice be given to the lowest achieving children from low-income families. As of the 2002-03 school year, school choice is available to students enrolled in schools that have been identified as needing improvement under the *ESEA* as the statute existed prior to the enactment of *No Child Left Behind*.

In addition, children are eligible for school choice when they attend any "persistently dangerous school," as defined by the individual state. Any child who has been the victim of a violent crime on the grounds of his or her school is also eligible for school choice.

How do parents know if their child is eligible for school choice?

Under *No Child Left Behind*, school districts are required to notify parents if their child is eligible for school choice because his or her school has been identified as needing improvement, corrective action or restructuring. They must notify parents no later than the first day of the school year following the year for which their school has been identified for improvement.

States are required to ensure that school choice is offered as an option to parents in the event their child is attending a school that is "persistently dangerous" or has been the victim of a violent crime while on school grounds.

What action can parents take if their school or district does not offer school choice to their child who is eligible?

Schools and districts receiving Title I funds must provide choice for eligible students as described above. If they do not, parents are encouraged to contact their state department of education.

Do public school options include only schools in the same district?

There may be situations where children in Title I schools have school options outside their own district. For instance, a school district may choose to enter into a cooperative agreement with another district that would allow their students to transfer into the other district's schools. In fact, the law requires that a district try "to the extent practicable" to establish such an agreement in the event that all of its schools have been identified as needing improvement, corrective action or restructuring.

Is transportation available for children who exercise their right to attend another school?

Subject to a funding cap established in the statute, districts must provide transportation for all students who exercise their school choice option under Title I. They must give priority to the lowest-achieving children from low-income families.

What are supplemental educational services?

Supplemental educational services include tutoring and after-school services. They may be offered through public- or private-sector providers that are approved by the state, such as public schools, public charter schools, local education agencies, educational service agencies and faith-based organizations. Private-sector providers may be either nonprofit or for-profit entities. States must maintain a list of approved providers across the state organized by the school district or districts they serve, from which parents may select (see Q-and-A below "Can parents choose providers for tutoring and other supplemental educational services?"). States must also promote maximum participation by supplemental educational services providers to ensure that parents have as many choices as possible.

When are children eligible to receive supplemental educational services?

Students from low-income families who remain in Title I schools that fail to meet state standards for at least three years are eligible to receive supplemental educational services.

Are parents notified about supplemental educational services?

Yes. Local education agencies are required to provide annual notice to parents of eligible children about the availability of services and information on the approved providers.

Can parents choose providers for tutoring and other supplemental educational services?

Yes, parents of eligible children can choose from the list of state-approved providers. Most states have approved a diverse list of providers, as mentioned above. Upon request, the local education agency will help parents determine which provider would best fit their child's needs. When parents have made their selection, the local education agency must then contract with that provider to deliver the services.

What action can parents take if their child is eligible for tutoring or other supplemental educational services, but their school or district does not offer them?

Districts receiving Title I funds must offer free tutoring and other extra help to eligible students, as described above. If eligible students are not being offered these services, parents are encouraged to contact their state department of education.

How are providers of supplemental educational services held accountable?

States must develop and apply objective criteria for evaluating providers and monitor the quality of services that they offer. In addition, supplemental services providers must give to parents, as well as to the school, information on their children's progress.

Charter Schools

What are charter schools and why are they named as a school-choice option under *No Child Left Behind*?

Charter schools are independent public schools designed and operated by parents, educators, community leaders, education entrepreneurs and others. They operate with a contract, or charter, from a public agency, such as a local or state education agency, an institution of higher education or a municipality. They must meet standards set forth in their charters for students and for the school as a whole, or else the chartering agency can close the school.

No Child Left Behind specifically names public charter schools as a school-choice option for children in schools that are identified for improvement, corrective action or restructuring, because they offer a viable alternative to public schools in the traditional system. In fact, the development of charter schools began in the 1990s as a means of providing expanded educational options for parents within the public school system. Today there are some 2,700 U.S. charter schools serving some 700,000 students nationwide.

Do all states have charter schools?

No. Currently only 39 states have public charter schools laws that provide this option for students. While some states have laws that strongly promote charter school growth, others do not. As a result, the situation varies among states, with thriving charter schools in some and very little or no charter-school activity in others. Parents may contact their local school district or state department of education to determine the availability of charter schools or to find out if there is a mechanism for starting such a school in their area.

How are charter schools held accountable under *No Child Left Behind?*

Although charter schools operate outside the traditional system, they are still accountable. The accountability provisions and other requirements of *No Child Left Behind* must be applied to charter schools in accordance with the states' charter school laws. State-authorized chartering agencies, as established by the individual state laws, are responsible for ensuring that charter schools meet the accountability and testing provisions of *No Child Left Behind*. In March 2003, the Department issued guidance on the impact of the new Title I requirements on charter schools, including details on accountability requirements (see Appendix A: Where to Go for More Information).

How can parents find out more about charter schools?

Parents interested in charter schools should contact their school district office or state education agency. More information is available through the Department's Web site given in Appendix A: Where to Go for More Information.

Appendix A

Where to Go for More Information

Federal Resources

For information on *No Child Left Behind* and the U.S. Department of Education, call toll-free at 1-800-USA-LEARN. Or check the first two Web sites given below.

>No Child Left Behind
>www.NoChildLeftBehind.gov

>U.S. Department of Education
>www.ed.gov

>The White House
>www.whitehouse.gov

State and Local Resources

>To locate a State Education Agency:
>http://nces.ed.gov/ccd/ccseas.html

>Note: The State Education Agency Web site should also provide links to local education agencies' Web sites.

>To locate a particular school, use the Nation-wide School Locator:
>http://nces.ed.gov/globallocator/

Topics

>Adequate Yearly Progress
>www.nclb.gov/start/facts/yearly.html

>Accountability
>www.nclb.gov/next/faqs/accountability.html

Charter Schools

> General Information:
> www.nclb.gov/start/facts/charter.html

> Guidance on Impact of New Title I on Charter Schools:
> http://www.ed.gov/offices/OII/choice/charterguidance03.pdf

> National Assessment of Educational Progress
> http://nces.ed.gov/nationsreportcard/

> National Reading Panel Report
> www.nationalreadingpanel.org/

> Reading First
> www.ed.gov/offices/OESE/readingfirst

> School Choice
> www.nclb.gov/next/faqs/choice.html#1

> Supplemental Educational Services
> www.nclb.gov/parents/supplementalservices/index.html

> What Works Clearinghouse on Education Research
> www.w-w-c.org

TV Program

> "Education News Parents Can Use"
> www.ed.gov/offices/OIIA/television/index.html

Appendix B

Titles of the *Elementary and Secondary Education Act of 1965*, as reauthorized by the *No Child Left Behind Act of 2001*

Note: The direct link to this legislation online is www.ed.gov/legislation/ESEA02/index.html. To access a title-by-title summary of the law, check www.ed.gov/offices/OESE/esea/progsum.
Also see http://thomas.loc.gov/bss/d107query.html (reference 107th Congress; PL 107-110).

Title I		Improving the Academic Achievement of the Disadvantaged
Title II		Preparing, Training and Recruiting High Quality Teachers and Principals
Title III		Language Instruction of Limited English Proficient and Immigrant Students
Title IV		21st Century Schools
Title V		Promoting Informed Parental Choice and Innovative Programs
Title VI		Flexibility and Accountability
Title VII		Indian, Native Hawaiian and Alaska Native Education
Title VIII		Impact Aid Program
Title IX		General Provisions

The *No Child Left Behind Act* also amended and reauthorized the education-related provisions of the *McKinney-Vento Homeless Assistance Act*. These provisions are also available on the Web site.

Appendix C

Key Sections of Title I—Improving the Academic Achievement of the Disadvantaged, Pertaining to Parent Involvement

- Section 1111(d) concerns parent involvement requirements for states.

- Section 1118 concerns parent involvement requirements for districts and schools. Because this provision of the law is so important to effective parent involvement, it is reprinted below.

- Section 1114 (b) (2) (B) (ii) concerns parent involvement requirements for schoolwide programs.

- Section 1120 (a) concerns parent involvement related to children enrolled in private schools.

Reprinted from Title I—Improving the Academic Achievement of the Disadvantaged

SEC. 1118. PARENTAL INVOLVEMENT.
    (a) LOCAL EDUCATIONAL AGENCY POLICY-
        (1) IN GENERAL- A local educational agency may receive funds under this part only if such agency implements programs, activities, and procedures for the involvement of parents in programs assisted under this part consistent with this section. Such programs, activities, and procedures shall be planned and implemented with meaningful consultation with parents of participating children.
        (2) WRITTEN POLICY- Each local educational agency that receives funds under this part shall develop jointly with, agree on with, and distribute to, parents of participating children a written parent involvement policy. The policy shall be incorporated into the local educational agency's plan developed under section 1112, establish the agency's expectations for parent involvement, and describe how the agency will —
            (A) involve parents in the joint development of the plan under section 1112, and the process of school review and improvement under section 1116;
            (B) provide the coordination, technical assistance, and other support necessary to assist participating schools in planning and implementing effective parent involvement activities to improve student academic achievement and school performance;
            (C) build the schools' and parents' capacity for strong parental involvement as described in subsection (e);

(D) coordinate and integrate parental involvement strategies under this part with parental involvement strategies under other programs, such as the Head Start program, Reading First program, Early Reading First program, Even Start program, Parents as Teachers program, and Home Instruction Program for Preschool Youngsters, and State-run preschool programs;

(E) conduct, with the involvement of parents, an annual evaluation of the content and effectiveness of the parental involvement policy in improving the academic quality of the schools served under this part, including identifying barriers to greater participation by parents in activities authorized by this section (with particular attention to parents who are economically disadvantaged, are disabled, have limited English proficiency, have limited literacy, or are of any racial or ethnic minority background), and use the findings of such evaluation to design strategies for more effective parental involvement, and to revise, if necessary, the parental involvement policies described in this section; and

(F) involve parents in the activities of the schools served under this part.

(3) RESERVATION-

(A) IN GENERAL- Each local educational agency shall reserve not less than 1 percent of such agency's allocation under subpart 2 of this part to carry out this section, including promoting family literacy and parenting skills, except that this paragraph shall not apply if 1 percent of such agency's allocation under subpart 2 of this part for the fiscal year for which the determination is made is $5,000 or less.

(B) PARENTAL INPUT- Parents of children receiving services under this part shall be involved in the decisions regarding how funds reserved under subparagraph (A) are allotted for parental involvement activities.

(C) DISTRIBUTION OF FUNDS- Not less than 95 percent of the funds reserved under subparagraph (A) shall be distributed to schools served under this part.

(b) SCHOOL PARENTAL INVOLVEMENT POLICY-

(1) IN GENERAL- Each school served under this part shall jointly develop with, and distribute to, parents of participating children a written parental involvement policy, agreed on by such parents, that shall describe the means for carrying out the requirements of subsections (c) through (f). Parents shall be notified of the policy in an understandable and uniform format and, to the extent practicable, provided in a language the parents can understand. Such policy shall be made available to the local community and updated periodically to meet the changing needs of parents and the school.

(2) SPECIAL RULE- If the school has a parental involvement policy that applies to all parents, such school may amend that policy, if necessary, to meet the requirements of this subsection.

(3) AMENDMENT- If the local educational agency involved has a school district-level parental involvement policy that applies to all parents, such agency may amend that policy, if necessary, to meet the requirements of this subsection.

(4) PARENTAL COMMENTS- If the plan under section 1112 is not satisfactory to the parents of participating children, the local educational agency shall submit any parent comments with such plan when such local educational agency submits the plan to the State.

(c) POLICY INVOLVEMENT- Each school served under this part shall —

(1) convene an annual meeting, at a convenient time, to which all parents of participating children shall be invited and encouraged to attend, to inform parents of their school's participation under this part and to explain the requirements of this part, and the right of the parents to be involved;

(2) offer a flexible number of meetings, such as meetings in the morning or evening, and may provide, with funds provided under this part, transportation, child care, or home visits, as such services relate to parental involvement;

(3) involve parents, in an organized, ongoing, and timely way, in the planning, review, and improvement of programs under this part, including the planning, review, and improvement of the school parental involvement policy and the joint development of the schoolwide program plan under section 1114(b)(2), except that if a school has in place a process for involving parents in the joint planning and design of the school's programs, the school may use that process, if such process includes an adequate representation of parents of participating children;

(4) provide parents of participating children —

(A) timely information about programs under this part;

(B) a description and explanation of the curriculum in use at the school, the forms of academic assessment used to measure student progress, and the proficiency levels students are expected to meet; and

(C) if requested by parents, opportunities for regular meetings to formulate suggestions and to participate, as appropriate, in decisions relating to the education of their children, and respond to any such suggestions as soon as practicably possible; and

(5) if the schoolwide program plan under section 1114(b)(2) is not satisfactory to the parents of participating children, submit any parent comments on the plan when the school makes the plan available to the local educational agency.

(d) SHARED RESPONSIBILITIES FOR HIGH STUDENT ACADEMIC ACHIEVEMENT- As a component of the school-level parental involvement policy developed under subsection (b), each school served under this part shall jointly develop with parents for all children served under this part a school-parent compact that outlines how parents, the entire school staff, and students will share the responsibility for improved student academic achievement and the means by which the school and parents will build and develop a partnership to help children achieve the State's high standards. Such compact shall —

(1) describe the school's responsibility to provide high-quality curriculum and instruction in a supportive and effective learning environment that enables the children served under this part to meet the State's student academic achievement standards, and the ways in which each parent will be responsible for supporting their children's learning, such as monitoring attendance, homework completion, and television watching; volunteering in their child's classroom; and participating, as appropriate, in decisions

relating to the education of their children and positive use of extracurricular time; and

(2) address the importance of communication between teachers and parents on an ongoing basis through, at a minimum —

    (A) parent-teacher conferences in elementary schools, at least annually, during which the compact shall be discussed as the compact relates to the individual child's achievement;

    (B) frequent reports to parents on their children's progress; and

    (C) reasonable access to staff, opportunities to volunteer and participate in their child's class, and observation of classroom activities.

(e) BUILDING CAPACITY FOR INVOLVEMENT- To ensure effective involvement of parents and to support a partnership among the school involved, parents, and the community to improve student academic achievement, each school and local educational agency assisted under this part —

(1) shall provide assistance to parents of children served by the school or local educational agency, as appropriate, in understanding such topics as the State's academic content standards and State student academic achievement standards, State and local academic assessments, the requirements of this part, and how to monitor a child's progress and work with educators to improve the achievement of their children;

(2) shall provide materials and training to help parents to work with their children to improve their children's achievement, such as literacy training and using technology, as appropriate, to foster parental involvement;

(3) shall educate teachers, pupil services personnel, principals, and other staff, with the assistance of parents, in the value and utility of contributions of parents, and in how to reach out to, communicate with, and work with parents as equal partners, implement and coordinate parent programs, and build ties between parents and the school;

(4) shall, to the extent feasible and appropriate, coordinate and integrate parent involvement programs and activities with Head Start, Reading First, Early Reading First, Even Start, the Home Instruction Programs for Preschool Youngsters, the Parents as Teachers Program, and public preschool and other programs, and conduct other activities, such as parent resource centers, that encourage and support parents in more fully participating in the education of their children;

(5) shall ensure that information related to school and parent programs, meetings, and other activities is sent to the parents of participating children in a format and, to the extent practicable, in a language the parents can understand;

(6) may involve parents in the development of training for teachers, principals, and other educators to improve the effectiveness of such training;

(7) may provide necessary literacy training from funds received under this part if the local educational agency has exhausted all other reasonably available sources of funding for such training;

(8) may pay reasonable and necessary expenses associated with local parental involvement activities, including transportation and child care costs, to enable parents to participate in school-related meetings and training sessions;

(9) may train parents to enhance the involvement of other parents;

(10) may arrange school meetings at a variety of times, or conduct in-home conferences between teachers or other educators, who work directly with participating children, with parents who are unable to attend such conferences at school, in order to maximize parental involvement and participation;

(11) may adopt and implement model approaches to improving parental involvement;

(12) may establish a districtwide parent advisory council to provide advice on all matters related to parental involvement in programs supported under this section;

(13) may develop appropriate roles for community-based organizations and businesses in parent involvement activities; and

(14) shall provide such other reasonable support for parental involvement activities under this section as parents may request.

(f) ACCESSIBILITY– In carrying out the parental involvement requirements of this part, local educational agencies and schools, to the extent practicable, shall provide full opportunities for the participation of parents with limited English proficiency, parents with disabilities, and parents of migratory children, including providing information and school reports required under section 1111 in a format and, to the extent practicable, in a language such parents understand.

(g) INFORMATION FROM PARENTAL INFORMATION AND RESOURCE CENTERS- In a State where a parental information and resource center is established to provide training, information, and support to parents and individuals who work with local parents, local educational agencies, and schools receiving assistance under this part, each local educational agency or school that receives assistance under this part and is located in the State shall assist parents and parental organizations by informing such parents and organizations of the existence and purpose of such centers.

(h) REVIEW- The State educational agency shall review the local educational agency's parental involvement policies and practices to determine if the policies and practices meet the requirements of this section.

Appendix D

Cited References

Eccles, J.S. and Harold, R.D. (1996) Family Involvement in Children's and Adolescents' Schooling. In *Family-School Links: How Do They Affect Educational Outcomes?* ed. A. Booth and J.F. Dunn, 3-34, Mahwah, N.J.: Lawrence Erlbaum Associates, Publishers.

National Center for Education Statistics. (2001) *The Nation's Report Card: Fourth-Grade Reading Highlights 2000.* Washington, D.C.: U.S. Department of Education.

National Center for Education Statistics. (2000) *NAEP 1999 Trends in Academic Progress: Three Decades of Student Performance.* Washington, D.C.: U.S. Department of Education.

National Reading Panel. (2000) *Report of the National Reading Panel—Teaching Children to Read: An Evidence-Based Assessment of the Scientific Research Literature on Reading and Its Implications for Reading Instruction.* Washington, D.C.: National Institute of Child Health and Human Development.

Sanders, W.L. and Rivers, J.C. (1996) *Cumulative and Residual Effects of Teachers on Future Student Academic Achievement.* Knoxville, Tenn., University of Tennessee. Retrieved from www.mdk12.org/instruction/ensure/tva/tva_2.html.

Snow, C.E., Burns, S. M., & Griffin, P. (Eds.). (1998) *Preventing Reading Difficulties in Young Children.* Washington, D.C.: National Academy Press.

Acknowledgments

The following employees of the U.S. Department of Education helped prepare this publication:

Beverley Blondell

Sandra Cook

Bill Cordes

Thomas Corwin

Thomas Dawson

Chris Doherty

Sandi Jacobs

C. Todd Jones

Lonna Jones

Marilyn Joyner

Todd Lamb

Stacey Lukens

Meredith Miller

Bill Modzeleski

Edward Ohnemus

Kathy Perkinson

Phil Rosenfelt

Robert Scott

Celia Sims

Jeffrey Sims

Thomas Skelly

Gretchen Slease

Ricky Takai

Christine Wolfe

John Woods

Jacquelyn Zimmermann